The UNITED STATES PRESIDENTS

James K. POLK

BreAnn Rumsch

Big Buddy Books

An Imprint of Abdo Publishing

abdopublishing.com

abdopublishing.com

Published by Abdo Publishing, a division of ABDO, PO Box 398166, Minneapolis, Minnesota 55439. Copyright © 2017 by Abdo Consulting Group, Inc. International copyrights reserved in all countries. No part of this book may be reproduced in any form without written permission from the publisher. Big Buddy Books™ is a trademark and logo of Abdo Publishing.

Printed in the United States of America, North Mankato, Minnesota
062016
092016

THIS BOOK CONTAINS
RECYCLED MATERIALS

Design: Sarah DeYoung, Mighty Media, Inc.
Production: Mighty Media, Inc.
Editor: Liz Salzmann
Cover Photograph: Getty
Interior Photographs: Alamy (p. 29); Corbis (pp. 5, 7, 25); Getty Images (pp. 6, 11, 19, 23); Library of
    Congress (pp. 13, 17, 21); North Wind (p. 27); Picture History (pp. 6, 15); Wikimedia Commons (p. 9)

Cataloging-in-Publication Data

Names: Rumsch, BreAnn, author.
Title: James K. Polk / by BreAnn Rumsch.
Description: Minneapolis, MN : Abdo Publishing, [2017] | Series: United States
    presidents | Includes bibliographical references and index.
Identifiers: LCCN 2015957500 | ISBN 9781680781137 (lib. bdg.) |
    ISBN 9781680775334 (ebook)
Subjects: LCSH: Polk, James K. (James Knox), 1795-1849--Juvenile literature. |
    Presidents--United States--Biography--Juvenile literature. | United States--
    Politics and government--1845-1849--Juvenile literature.
Classification: DDC 973.6/1092 [B]--dc23
LC record available at http://lccn.loc.gov/2015957500

Contents

James K. Polk 4

Timeline 6

Tennessee Youth 8

Starting Out 10

Entering Politics 12

Dark Horse 16

President Polk 20

Oregon Treaty 22

War with Mexico 24

Polk Place 28

Office of the President 30

Presidents and Their Terms 34

Glossary 38

Websites 39

Index 40

James K. Polk

James K. Polk was the eleventh president of the United States. As president, he created an independent **treasury**. Polk also established the border between the Oregon country and Canada. And, he led the United States in a war against Mexico.

During his presidency, Polk helped the country gain more than 500,000 square miles (1.3 million sq km) of land. By the end of Polk's term, the United States went from coast to coast.

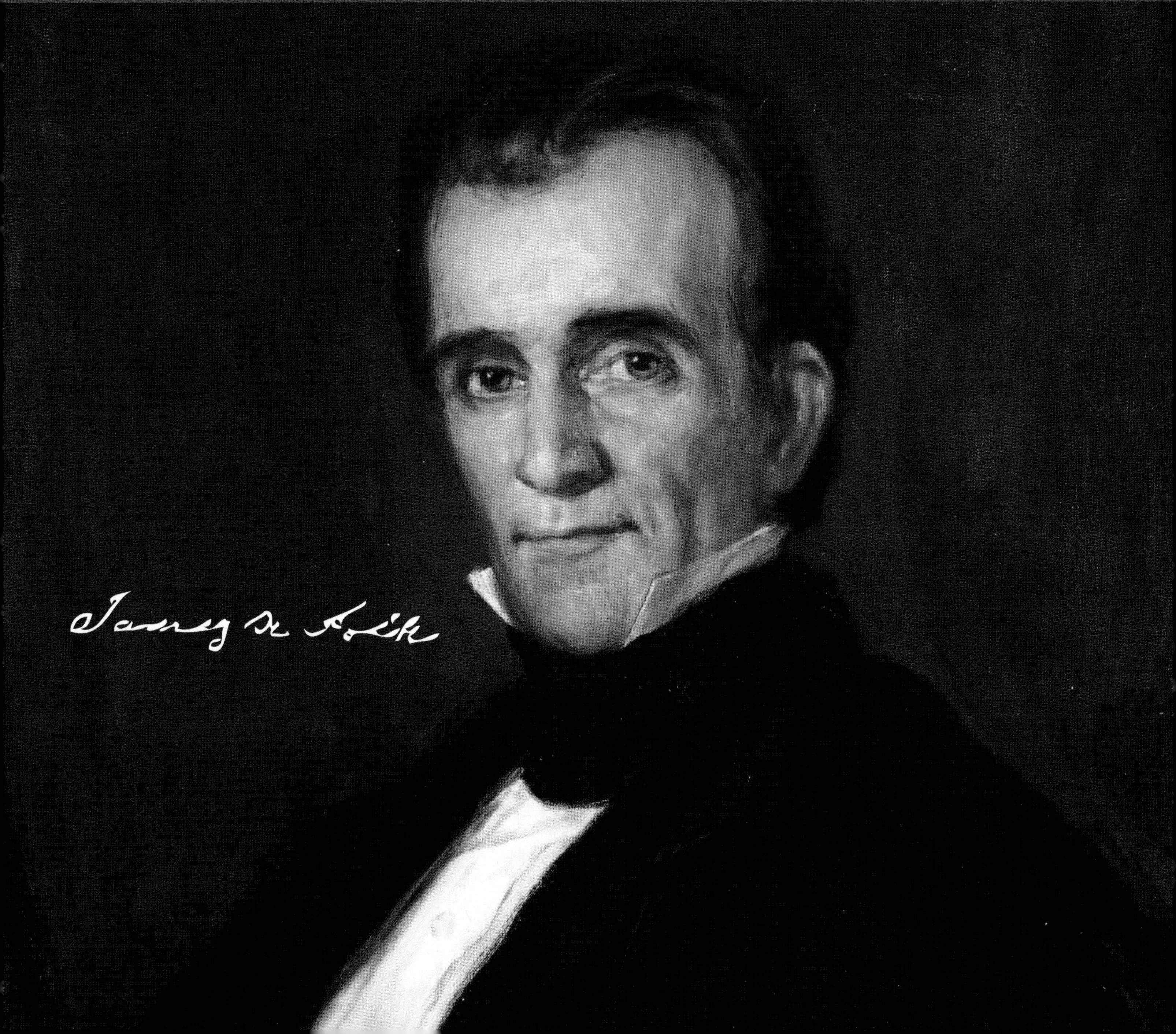
James K. Polk

Timeline

1795

On November 2, James Knox Polk was born in Mecklenburg County, North Carolina.

1824

On January 1, Polk married Sarah Childress.

1823

Polk won election to the Tennessee House of **Representatives**.

1825

Polk won election to the US House of Representatives.

1845

On March 4, Polk became the eleventh US president.

1839

Polk became governor of Tennessee.

1849

On June 15, James K. Polk died at his home in Nashville, Tennessee.

7

Tennessee Youth

James Knox Polk was born on November 2, 1795, in Mecklenburg County, North Carolina. When James was 11, his family moved to Columbia, Tennessee.

James attended the University of North Carolina. He **graduated** in 1818.

The only surviving Polk family home stands in Columbia, Tennessee. James lived in the house from 1818 to 1824.

Starting Out

After **graduation**, Polk decided to become a **lawyer**. He moved to Nashville, Tennessee. There, he began working for Felix Grundy. Grundy helped Polk become a clerk in the Tennessee state senate in 1819.

Polk also kept studying to be a lawyer. In 1820, Polk passed his lawyer's test. He then returned to Columbia and opened his own law firm.

About this time, Polk met Sarah Childress. The couple married on January 1, 1824.

Sarah Childress was the daughter of a successful businessman.

Entering Politics

Meanwhile, Polk decided to run for the Tennessee House of **Representatives**. He won the election in 1823. As a Tennessee representative, Polk worked to lower taxes and improve state schools.

In 1825, Polk ran for the US House of Representatives. He won, and left Tennessee for Washington, DC. In 1828, Polk helped Andrew Jackson campaign for president. Jackson won and took office the following year. In Congress, Polk agreed with President Jackson's ideas.

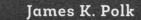

Andrew Jackson was president from 1829 to 1837.

In 1835, Polk became **Speaker of the House**. As Speaker, Polk worked to keep order in the House. This was very important during arguments about slavery.

Polk believed Congress had no authority to act on slavery. He thought each state should decide individually whether to allow slavery. Polk served as Speaker until 1839.

Then, Jackson talked him into running for governor of Tennessee. Polk won the election. He served as governor from 1839 to 1841.

★ DID YOU KNOW? ★

Polk was reelected to the US House of **Representatives** six times.

In his 14 years of service, Polk only missed going to Congress once.

Dark Horse

Polk decided to return to national **politics**. At the 1844 **Democratic National Convention**, the **Democrats** could not agree on a **candidate** for president. They voted seven times. But no candidate received enough votes to be **nominated**.

Then, they added Polk as a candidate. It took two more votes, but finally one candidate got enough votes to be nominated. It was Polk!

Polk's nomination came as a surprise. So, he became known as the dark horse candidate.

George M. Dallas of Pennsylvania was chosen as Polk's vice president.

The **Whig Party** chose Henry Clay to run for president. Clay had served in the US House of **Representatives** and the US Senate. He had also been **secretary of state** under President John Quincy Adams.

Clay was against Texas becoming a state. But Polk was for it. Polk also wanted to claim part of the Oregon Territory from British control.

Polk made sure Americans heard his ideas. Many people agreed with Polk. The Whigs tried hard to beat him. Yet Polk won the election!

★ DID YOU KNOW? ★

During Polk's presidency, the US Naval Academy was founded in Annapolis, Maryland.

Henry Clay

President Polk

Polk became president on March 4, 1845. As president, one of his plans was to lower **tariffs**. Polk's **secretary of the treasury**, Robert J. Walker, wrote a new tariff. In 1846, Congress passed the Walker Tariff Act. The act lowered tariffs on some things brought from other countries. This was the first tariff written by the **executive branch**.

★ SUPREME COURT ★
APPOINTMENTS

Levi Woodbury: 1845

Robert C. Grier: 1846

Hundreds of people stood in the rain to watch Polk become president.

Oregon Treaty

Back in 1818, England and the United States had signed a **treaty**. In it, they agreed to share the Oregon country. This area included land between present-day Alaska and California.

Now, many congressmen wanted the United States to claim part of the land. So in 1846, Polk and **Secretary of State** James Buchanan made a deal with England.

That year, the two countries signed the Oregon Treaty. It set the border at the forty-ninth **parallel**.

James
Buchanan

War with Mexico

Texas had become a state in December 1845. But Mexico still wanted to control Texas. The two nations also disagreed about where the state's border should be.

President Polk sent Congressman John Slidell to settle the Texas border disagreement. But the Mexican officials refused to meet with Slidell. So in January 1846, Polk sent US troops to Texas.

On April 25, Mexican soldiers attacked the American troops. On May 13, Congress announced a war against Mexico.

PRESIDENT POLK'S CABINET

March 4, 1845–March 4, 1849

- ★ **STATE:** James Buchanan
- ★ **TREASURY:** Robert J. Walker
- ★ **WAR:** William Learned Marcy
- ★ **NAVY:** George Bancroft,
  John Young Mason (from September 9, 1846)
- ★ **ATTORNEY GENERAL:** John Young Mason,
  Nathan Clifford (from October 17, 1846),
  Isaac Toucey (from June 29, 1848)

The **Mexican-American War** continued for two years. It ended on February 2, 1848. That's when both countries signed the **Treaty** of Guadalupe Hidalgo.

Through the treaty, Mexico agreed to give up its claim to Texas and other land in the west in return for $15 million. The border between the United States and Mexico was set at the Rio Grande.

Today, the land the Unites States received makes up California, Nevada, and Utah. It also includes parts of Arizona, New Mexico, Colorado, and Wyoming.

The yellow area on this map shows the part of Texas that sparked the Mexican-American War.

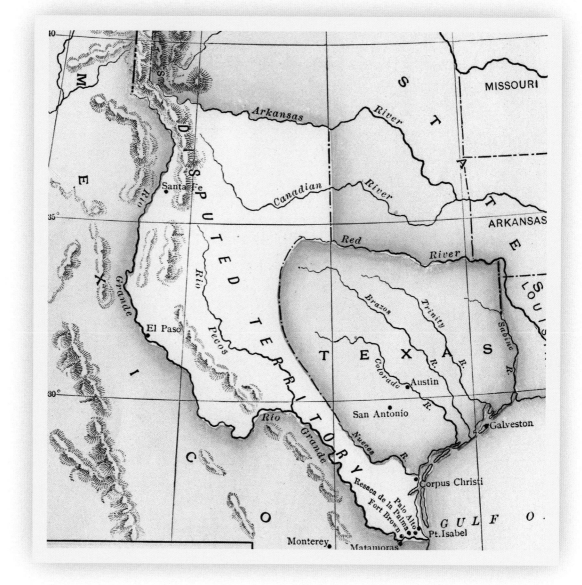

Polk Place

At the end of his term, Polk refused to run for reelection. Polk was the first US president to not seek a second term. In 1849, Polk and his wife returned to Nashville, Tennessee. Their home was called Polk Place.

On the journey, Polk became sick. He never got better. On June 15, 1849, James K. Polk died. Sarah Polk died in 1891.

James K. Polk was an honest **politician**. He worked hard to be a strong leader for his country.

The Polks are buried together in Nashville, Tennessee.

Office of the President

Branches of Government

The US government has three branches. They are the executive, legislative, and judicial branches. Each branch has some power over the others. This is called a system of checks and balances.

★ Executive Branch

The executive branch enforces laws. It is made up of the president, the vice president, and the president's cabinet. The president represents the United States around the world. He or she also signs bills into law and leads the military.

★ Legislative Branch

The legislative branch makes laws, maintains the military, and regulates trade. It also has the power to declare war. This branch includes the Senate and the House of Representatives. Together, these two houses form Congress.

★ Judicial Branch

The judicial branch interprets laws. It is made up of district courts, courts of appeals, and the Supreme Court. District courts try cases. Sometimes people disagree with a trial's outcome. Then he or she may appeal. If a court of appeals supports the ruling, a person may appeal to the Supreme Court.

Qualifications for Office

To be president, a candidate must be at least 35 years old. The person must be a natural-born US citizen. He or she must also have lived in the United States for at least 14 years.

Electoral College

The US presidential election is an indirect election. Voters from each state choose electors. These electors represent their state in the Electoral College. Each elector has one electoral vote. Electors cast their vote for the candidate with the highest number of votes from people in their state. A candidate must receive the majority of Electoral College votes to win.

Term of Office

Each president may be elected to two four-year terms. The presidential election is held on the Tuesday after the first Monday in November. The president is sworn in on January 20 of the following year. At that time, he or she takes the oath of office.
It states:

> I do solemnly swear (or affirm) that I will faithfully execute the office of President of the United States, and will to the best of my ability, preserve, protect and defend the Constitution of the United States.

31

Line of Succession

The Presidential Succession Act of 1947 states who becomes president if the president cannot serve. The vice president is first in the line. Next are the Speaker of the House and the President Pro Tempore of the Senate. It may happen that none of these individuals is able to serve. Then the office falls to the president's cabinet members. They would take office in the order in which each department was created:

Secretary of State

Secretary of the Treasury

Secretary of Defense

Attorney General

Secretary of the Interior

Secretary of Agriculture

Secretary of Commerce

Secretary of Labor

Secretary of Health and Human Services

Secretary of Housing and Urban Development

Secretary of Transportation

Secretary of Energy

Secretary of Education

Secretary of Veterans Affairs

Secretary of Homeland Security

Benefits

★ While in office, the president receives a salary. It is $400,000 per year. He or she lives in the White House. The president also has 24-hour Secret Service protection.

★ The president may travel on a Boeing 747 jet. This special jet is called Air Force One. It can hold 70 passengers. It has kitchens, a dining room, sleeping areas, and more. Air Force One can fly halfway around the world before needing to refuel. It can even refuel in flight!

★ When the president travels by car, he or she uses Cadillac One. It is a Cadillac Deville that has been modified. The car has heavy armor and communications systems. The president may even take Cadillac One along when visiting other countries.

★ The president also travels on a helicopter. It is called Marine One. It may also be taken along when the president visits other countries.

★ Sometimes the president needs to get away with family and friends. Camp David is the official presidential retreat. It is located in Maryland. The US Navy maintains the retreat. The US Marine Corps keeps it secure. The camp offers swimming, tennis, golf, and hiking.

★ When the president leaves office, he or she receives lifetime Secret Service protection. He or she also receives a yearly pension of $203,700. The former president also receives money for office space, supplies, and staff.

PRESIDENTS AND THEIR TERMS

PRESIDENT	PARTY	TOOK OFFICE	LEFT OFFICE	TERMS SERVED	VICE PRESIDENT
George Washington	None	April 30, 1789	March 4, 1797	Two	John Adams
John Adams	Federalist	March 4, 1797	March 4, 1801	One	Thomas Jefferson
Thomas Jefferson	Democratic-Republican	March 4, 1801	March 4, 1809	Two	Aaron Burr, George Clinton
James Madison	Democratic-Republican	March 4, 1809	March 4, 1817	Two	George Clinton, Elbridge Gerry
James Monroe	Democratic-Republican	March 4, 1817	March 4, 1825	Two	Daniel D. Tompkins
John Quincy Adams	Democratic-Republican	March 4, 1825	March 4, 1829	One	John C. Calhoun
Andrew Jackson	Democrat	March 4, 1829	March 4, 1837	Two	John C. Calhoun, Martin Van Buren
Martin Van Buren	Democrat	March 4, 1837	March 4, 1841	One	Richard M. Johnson
William H. Harrison	Whig	March 4, 1841	April 4, 1841	Died During First Term	John Tyler
John Tyler	Whig	April 6, 1841	March 4, 1845	Completed Harrison's Term	Office Vacant
James K. Polk	Democrat	March 4, 1845	March 4, 1849	One	George M. Dallas
Zachary Taylor	Whig	March 5, 1849	July 9, 1850	Died During First Term	Millard Fillmore

PRESIDENT	PARTY	TOOK OFFICE	LEFT OFFICE	TERMS SERVED	VICE PRESIDENT
Millard Fillmore	Whig	July 10, 1850	March 4, 1853	Completed Taylor's Term	Office Vacant
Franklin Pierce	Democrat	March 4, 1853	March 4, 1857	One	William R.D. King
James Buchanan	Democrat	March 4, 1857	March 4, 1861	One	John C. Breckinridge
Abraham Lincoln	Republican	March 4, 1861	April 15, 1865	Served One Term, Died During Second Term	Hannibal Hamlin, Andrew Johnson
Andrew Johnson	Democrat	April 15, 1865	March 4, 1869	Completed Lincoln's Second Term	Office Vacant
Ulysses S. Grant	Republican	March 4, 1869	March 4, 1877	Two	Schuyler Colfax, Henry Wilson
Rutherford B. Hayes	Republican	March 3, 1877	March 4, 1881	One	William A. Wheeler
James A. Garfield	Republican	March 4, 1881	September 19, 1881	Died During First Term	Chester Arthur
Chester Arthur	Republican	September 20, 1881	March 4, 1885	Completed Garfield's Term	Office Vacant
Grover Cleveland	Democrat	March 4, 1885	March 4, 1889	One	Thomas A. Hendricks
Benjamin Harrison	Republican	March 4, 1889	March 4, 1893	One	Levi P. Morton
Grover Cleveland	Democrat	March 4, 1893	March 4, 1897	One	Adlai E. Stevenson
William McKinley	Republican	March 4, 1897	September 14, 1901	Served One Term, Died During Second Term	Garret A. Hobart, Theodore Roosevelt

PRESIDENT	PARTY	TOOK OFFICE	LEFT OFFICE	TERMS SERVED	VICE PRESIDENT
Theodore Roosevelt	Republican	September 14, 1901	March 4, 1909	Completed McKinley's Second Term, Served One Term	Office Vacant, Charles Fairbanks
William Taft	Republican	March 4, 1909	March 4, 1913	One	James S. Sherman
Woodrow Wilson	Democrat	March 4, 1913	March 4, 1921	Two	Thomas R. Marshall
Warren G. Harding	Republican	March 4, 1921	August 2, 1923	Died During First Term	Calvin Coolidge
Calvin Coolidge	Republican	August 3, 1923	March 4, 1929	Completed Harding's Term, Served One Term	Office Vacant, Charles Dawes
Herbert Hoover	Republican	March 4, 1929	March 4, 1933	One	Charles Curtis
Franklin D. Roosevelt	Democrat	March 4, 1933	April 12, 1945	Served Three Terms, Died During Fourth Term	John Nance Garner, Henry A. Wallace, Harry S. Truman
Harry S. Truman	Democrat	April 12, 1945	January 20, 1953	Completed Roosevelt's Fourth Term, Served One Term	Office Vacant, Alben Barkley
Dwight D. Eisenhower	Republican	January 20, 1953	January 20, 1961	Two	Richard Nixon
John F. Kennedy	Democrat	January 20, 1961	November 22, 1963	Died During First Term	Lyndon B. Johnson
Lyndon B. Johnson	Democrat	November 22, 1963	January 20, 1969	Completed Kennedy's Term, Served One Term	Office Vacant, Hubert H. Humphrey
Richard Nixon	Republican	January 20, 1969	August 9, 1974	Completed First Term, Resigned During Second Term	Spiro T. Agnew, Gerald Ford

PRESIDENT	PARTY	TOOK OFFICE	LEFT OFFICE	TERMS SERVED	VICE PRESIDENT
Gerald Ford	Republican	August 9, 1974	January 20, 1977	Completed Nixon's Second Term	Nelson A. Rockefeller
Jimmy Carter	Democrat	January 20, 1977	January 20, 1981	One	Walter Mondale
Ronald Reagan	Republican	January 20, 1981	January 20, 1989	Two	George H.W. Bush
George H.W. Bush	Republican	January 20, 1989	January 20, 1993	One	Dan Quayle
Bill Clinton	Democrat	January 20, 1993	January 20, 2001	Two	Al Gore
George W. Bush	Republican	January 20, 2001	January 20, 2009	Two	Dick Cheney
Barack Obama	Democrat	January 20, 2009	January 20, 2017	Two	Joe Biden

"No President who performs his duty faithfully and conscientiously can have any leisure." James K. Polk

★ WRITE TO THE PRESIDENT ★

You may write to the president at:
The White House
1600 Pennsylvania Avenue NW
Washington, DC 20500

You may e-mail the president at:
comments@whitehouse.gov

Glossary

candidate (KAN-duh-dayt)—a person who seeks a political office.

Democrat—a member of the Democratic political party.

Democratic National Convention—a meeting during which the Democratic Party chooses candidates for president and vice president.

executive branch—the part of the government in charge of enforcing the country's laws.

graduate (GRA-juh-wayt)—to complete a level of schooling.

lawyer (LAW-yuhr)—a person who gives people advice on laws or represents them in court.

Mexican-American War—a war between the United States and Mexico that lasted from 1846 to 1848.

nominate—to name as a possible winner.

parallel—one of the imaginary lines around the earth that mark how far north or south things are.

politics—the art or science of government. Something referring to politics is political. A person who is active in politics is a politician.

representative—someone chosen in an election to act or speak for the people who voted for him or her.

secretary of state—a member of the president's cabinet who handles relations with other countries.

secretary of the treasury—a member of the president's cabinet who handles the nation's finances.

Speaker of the House—the highest-ranking member of the party with the majority in Congress.

tariff—the taxes a government puts on imported or exported goods.

treasury—a place where money is kept.

treaty—an agreement made between two or more groups.

Whig Party—a US political party active between 1834 and 1854.

★ WEBSITES ★

To learn more about the US Presidents, visit **booklinks.abdopublishing.com**. These links are routinely monitored and updated to provide the most current information available.

Index

Adams, John Quincy   **18**

Alaska   **22**

birth   **6, 8**

Buchanan, James   **22, 23, 25**

California   **22, 26**

Canada   **4**

Clay, Henry   **18, 19**

death   **7, 8, 28**

Democratic Party   **16**

education   **8, 10**

England   **22**

executive branch   **20**

family   **6, 8, 9, 10, 11, 28**

governor   **7, 14**

Grundy, Felix   **10**

House of Representatives   **6, 12, 14, 18**

Jackson, Andrew   **12, 13, 14**

law   **10**

Mexican-American War   **4, 24, 26, 27**

Oregon Territory   **4, 18, 22**

Rio Grande   **26, 27**

secretary of state   **18, 22**

slavery   **14**

Slidell, John   **24**

Speaker of the House   **14**

Tennessee   **7, 8, 9, 10, 12, 14, 28, 29**

Texas   **18, 24, 26, 27**

treasury   **4, 20**

Treaty of Guadalupe Hidalgo   **26**

Walker Tariff Act   **20**

Washington, DC   **12**

Whig Party   **18**